ARE YOU ON THE RIGHT TRACK?

Leslie Guity

B K
ROYSTON
Publishing

BK Royston Publishing
http://www.bkroystonpublishing.com
bkroystonpublishing@gmail.com

© Copyright – 2023

Cover Design: Leslie Guity

ISBN-13: 978-1-959543-48-0

Printed in the United States of America

Dedication

To those who are questioning their life direction, who are coasting on ordinary, who keep jumping from one track to another, who are just settling for okay, who are hanging on to past traumas, who don't know what their purpose is, who feel stuck, unloved, and hopeless, this book is dedicated to you.

This book is also dedicated to the ones I love.

Acknowledgements

I would like to thank and acknowledge my sister Tania Guity, who I bounce ideas off of or read my creations to. Even when she is busy, she appeases me.

She helps me in all aspects of my business, including making my business cards and the like. I really appreciate her.

I would also like to acknowledge my "daughter" Monet Johnson. She is a strong individual. She also helps me a lot. As I minister to her, I don't know if she knows how much she ministers to me.

And I would also like to mention my beautiful sista, sista, Gina Fernandes. She has been my friend since 6th grade. And she is still in my life. I am blessed to have a sistership for that long. She has my back at all times and I, hers.

For the most part, it was conversations with God that allowed me to write this book, but he did allow these three beautiful souls to assist, take a listen and be there for me during my creative mode.

I also want to mention Mitzi Spencer Carrasquillo, who God brought back to my life to make a difference in young girls lives one girl at a time. Miracles have been happening in the workshops that we present together. What a blessing!

I would also like to thank Richard Johnson, Daryl Braithwaite and Kelly Brown-Barrows who answered the questions," What did you want to be when you grew up?" What kept you for being what you dreamed of being?" and "What are you doing now?" These questions were asked during the early part of the writing process. I really appreciate your input. It is nice to hear other peoples' stories and tracks. Thank you.

I'd like to thank each and every one of you from the bottom of my heart.

Table of Contents

I Am Becoming

Born into the world, a black girl,

Of parents of Honduran descent.

Father came to soil foreign to him,

Long ago, not recent,

To make a home for his family.

What bravery!!!

Here I am, one who was created by God,

came into being via my mother's belly,

Filled with purpose already.

Growing up, having to deal with bullying,

Racism, low self-esteem and medical issues.

Can't see, can't breathe, can't stand up straight,

They told me I can't have babies.

Have vivid dreams, can read people's mind.

Grew up knowing I was one of a kind.

I am Becoming!

I can see sickness and disease.

I know liars and deceivers, and they know me and

Back away from me.

I can feel babies coming and also smell death.

Like an ugly duckling to a swan,

Like a caterpillar to a butterfly,

I am Becoming!

Highly sensitive because of the lightning bolt

Shooting through my body.

Rays of sunshine in, out and around me.

The misunderstood...

The misunderstood...

The misunderstood...

Music playing in my inner being,

A constant drumbeat, words,

Violins, harps, the trumpet sound.

Piano playing inside me, so I go

And touch the piano keys.

I am Becoming!

Languages in my spirit:

Spanish, speaking in other tongues,

Haitian and Cape Verde Creole,

Translating for all.

Dancing around, causing walls to fall.

Watch out, y'all!

Because I am Becoming!

Rivers and streams

Flowing out of me.

Visions and Dreams

Are coming to be.

Spinning world,

Nut and squirrel.

Spiritual gifts God gave

To every boy and girl.

Understanding the animals.

Understanding the swaying of the trees.

Adequate is not me.

I'm extraordinary.

I am Becoming!

Don't mean to boast,

Don't mean to offend.

Just trying to ride this thing called life

Gracefully to the end,

Doing all that God intends for me to do.

Cuz, I AM BECOMING!!!!

My Prayer

Dear God in Heaven,

 Bless this book. Give me the words to write to your people. Let this book help to lead them toward their prospective purposes and destination. Please don't allow my own thoughts nor my own will to be written in this book. Let the words written on these pages be straight from You.

I pray that after reading this book, people will be able to look back into their lives and see signs, patterns and gifts that would help them identify the track toward their purpose.

I pray that they will make healthy choices in all aspects of their lives. I pray that those people who are on the wrong track will find and board the train on the right track.

I also pray that they find the right direction and that their lives will drastically improve.

Amen

Introduction

The idea to write this book came as I sat at South Station, the largest train depot in Boston, Massachusetts. In the middle of the station, there is a gigantic digital departure board which tells you what track your train will be departing from and the departure time. They also announce train track information and departure times over the intercom.

When I get on my train, there are always people—and I mean always—people who should have boarded another train on board, despite the gigantic departure board and onboard audio announcements. When the train departs, people are going around asking passengers on the train where the train is going. They are not on the right track.

How did they manage to get on the wrong track when there are signs everywhere to tell them the track that their train was boarding?

Then I thought metaphorically, are we on the right track in life? Are we going where we are destined to be going? Are we doing what we are supposed to be doing? Or, are we like people who get on the wrong train asking passengers the train's destination?

The purpose of this book is not to condemn or to judge but for awareness purposes. There are tracks that the choices we make put us on, and then there are tracks that we are supposed to be on. Hopefully, they are one in the same.

What did you want to be when you grew up? Are you what you dreamed you would be? If not, why? Is it because you were scared? Did someone tell you that your dream was impossible? Did someone you trust talk you out of your dream? Did you just settle?

This book is to make you aware of different emotions and/or distractions and other obstacles which may have taken you off the right track.

The good thing about life is that if you are on the wrong track, you will always have the opportunity to get on the right one.

We were put on this earth to fulfill a purpose. There are people who are depending on us to get it right.

Please understand that the choices you make affect other people. Let's make sure you are on the right track and that you find your purpose. Are you ready to find the track that your train is on?

Let's go!

I mentioned above that there are signs everywhere. Here is an example of signs I received in making a difficult decision.

Let me tell you a story:

COVID VACCINE

I was not getting that shot. I repeat, I was not getting that shot. The government had mandated the vaccination, threatening suspension and termination of my job.

I said to myself, I guess I will be jobless and homeless.

I was going to try for medical waiver, but my doctor said that I was not allergic to anything in the shot.

I was going to go for religious reasons, but I could not find anything in the Bible that says that taking the vaccine goes against any Godly principles.

Besides, my pastors, whom I am accountable to, took the shot.

By the time I was moving toward getting the vaccine, it was too late to get the vaccinations that required two shots because the second shot would have been after the mandated deadline. I did not want to get the shot anyway, so why not take the vaccine which only consisted of one dose—one and done.

I made a vaccine shot appointment and pretty much prayed until the point of getting the shot.

I attempted to make an appointment on the government website. The website said that various locations had the one dose vaccine, but when I called those locations, I was told that they did not have that vaccine. The website was not updated.

I was then given the phone number to the resource line to make the appointment. I called the resource line on a Sunday. They made the appointment, but they advised me to call the facility the next day, to make sure they had the one dose vaccine.

I called the facility the next day to make sure that they had the vaccine, and a lady named Grace answered the phone.

This was my first sign that it would be okay to get the vaccine. God sent Grace.

I continued praying all week, reading the Word, trying to educate myself about the vaccine. I was still in the valley of decision. (I really did not want to get this vaccine.)

You see, in the past, I had taken the pneumonia vaccine and, six months later, caught the pneumonia so severely, it had me down for a whole month, not being able to breathe without feeling like someone was literally stabbing me in my back. This was one of the reasons that I was resistant about getting the COVID vaccine.

I asked a family member, who was against the vaccine, why was she against it. She sent me videos but I never got a chance to watch them because my life is so demanding.

I posted on social media that I had a big decision to make. The second sign came when a friend of mine commented on my generic post: What God has given, He will allow to flow through you. Be a vessel.

What? This was the same word that my pastor had said in his sermon on the same day. He said whether you get vaccinated or not, God will protect you. (He did not know that I was going to get the vaccine that day, either.)

The day came, and my sister, Tania, had volunteered to take me to my appointment. (I was still borderline freaking out.) I told her that the number of the facility's street address was 1014 and my appointment was at 1pm. When we arrived at that address, it was incorrect. Dyslexia had kicked in; I had transposed the numbers. The correct address number was 4110.

We were thirty minutes away from the destination and we were already fifteen minutes late.

I called the facility to inform them of my mistake. Isaiah answered the phone and said I could still come in.

That was the third sign.

When we made it to the parking lot, I received a call from the facility. I told them I would be right in.

I had taken Tylenol before the appointment. I prayed that I would not get any side effects. Guess what?

NO side effects.

Why did I tell this story? There were two different tracks that I could have taken. One track was to not get the vaccination and risk being jobless and homeless or take the vaccine and keep my job and home.

You see, there were signs that I was going to be okay if I took the shot.

In summary: The first sign was that Grace answered the phone. (God sent Grace). The second sign was that I posted on social media that I had a big decision to make. My friend commented that no matter what you put inside your body, God will protect you. She said that what is meant for evil, God will turn it around for good. She did not even know I was talking about getting vaccinated. And my pastor preached the same word on the very day I was to get vaccinated.

Then there was the third sign, when I discovered that the correct address number was 4110, and when I called to informed the clinic of the mix-up that led to my tardiness, Isaiah answered the phone.

You see, that was a clear sign, because Isaiah 41:10 in the Bible reads, 'So do not fear, for I am with you; do not be dismayed, for I am your God. I will strengthen you and help you; I will uphold you with your righteous hand'.

So let me repeat myself. I had no side effects, none. If, after those three signs, I had decided not to get the shot, would I have been disobedient? Maybe.

Some would beg to differ about my choice of receiving the vaccine, but based on the signs I received, I believe that I am on the right track.

Look at your past major decisions. Were there signs that led you to the resolution? Did you look at the gigantic board, like the one in South Station? Based on the signs that I presented, what track would you have taken? It will be interesting to know how others would decide their track.

Picture this: we are in South Station waiting for our prospective trains. There is a big, gigantic board that will tell us what track our prospective train is on. There is also an intercom shouting announcements.

LISTEN FOR THE TRACK THAT YOUR TRAIN IS ON TO BE CALLED!!!

"ATTENTION, PASSENGERS: The next train is on Track 1."

Track 1 – KEEP THE FAITH

```
 . . . . . . . . . . . . . . . . . . .
||||||||||||||||||||||||||
 . . . . . . . . . . . . . . . . . . .
```

I asked God what faith is.

There are other definitions, but I will use this one.

"Faith is the confidence in someone or something or a concept, even though we may not see the outcome."

We all have faith in something. We get on a plane, in hopes that we get to our destination. We eat out at restaurants, having faith that the food will taste good and that they will not give us food poisoning. We sit on a chair, having faith that the chair will hold us.

Let me tell you a little story about a chair. I was over at my sister's house. I sat on the plastic chair in front of the computer. No one expected what was about to happen next.

The chair's back legs gave way and broke, and next thing I knew, I fell backwards. I ended up still seated in the chair staring up at the ceiling.

I told you that story because it was funny... I was okay.

I had faith that the chair was going to hold me and it did hold me. I was still in the seat, even though I was facing the wrong way (upward); it did not hold me in the way I thought it would, but it held me.

Even though you have faith, things will not always go the way you think they will go.

Do we even know what and where our life track is? There is a gigantic digital board to tell you what track our train is on. There is also an audio system intercom that will tell you where to go, which is your inner voice, an inkling, or what I call the Holy Spirit.

I ask again, are you on the right track? What did you want to be when you grew up? Are you what you wanted to become? Or was your faith rattled to the point where you either went backwards, stopped in your tracks, or went in a different direction?

I was on the correct train at South Station, but am I on the right life track? "Faith moves mountains" is what we say, but do we really believe that? For a while, I did not.

What did I want to be when I grew up? I wanted to be a famous singer. I remember when I was on the Community Auditions TV show, I told Dave Maynard that I was a singing secretary. LOL.

I used to have dreams of singing and the audience forgetting about their problems just for a few hours. I did not become that famous singer with platinum records.

I had a baby, which changed the track of my life. I decided to work and go to school for advanced career development so that I might acquire a job that paid well enough to be able to raise a child—food, shelter, clothing, daycare etc. My love for my bundle of joy changed my track.

I went on to have four more children and was raising them as a single parent. If someone would have told me when I was young that I was going to have five children, I would not have believed them. I did sing in choirs, church worship teams, soloed for weddings and funerals... sang to put food on the table, and I still sing because singing is breathing to me, but I was/am on a different track.

Did anyone see the Indiana Jones movie, when he was following a map? Let's say the map was information on how to stay on track.

The map said that there was a bridge. He looked where the map said there was a bridge, and all he saw was a gaping hole. He looked at the map again and saw the bridge on it but not in front of him.

He had faith in the map as if it were the Bible. He stuck his foot out over the gaping hole and out came a piece of a bridge. Every step he took, another piece of the bridge appeared, until he was over to the other side.

If he did not trust the map, would he have stayed on the original side that he was on, and not have fulfilled what he needed to do on the other side? Would he have turned around and went to the starting point?

I, like Indiana Jones, would have stuck my foot out over the gaping hole, because if the map was the Bible, I believe what the Bible says. It says that God will make a way where there is no way and that He orders our steps if we let Him.

See, Indiana Jones stepped out; faith without works is dead.

Let me ask you a question. In the Indiana Jones scenario, would you have stepped out on faith and believed what the map said, or would you have stayed on the original side?

Your decision will decide whether or not you are on the right track. Faith is actually exercised when we are dealing with something beyond what we can comprehend. In order to live this life, we must have unwavering faith.

An example is when the pandemic shut down the whole world, we did not know what our fate was. We had to have faith that we were going to make it to the next season of our lives. The key is not to doubt. You are to rest assured that God will move on your behalf.

Sometimes God will tell you to do something that might sound crazy to you or go somewhere you would not normally go. Do it anyway. Obedience is better than sacrifice. There is a blessing in it.

Faith is not supposed to make sense; it is supposed to make faith. This is a quote my pastor preached one Sunday. Sometimes God will allow you to be on the wrong track so you can encourage others to get on the right track.

I recently watched a movie about a man who went to jail, taking the fall for a friend. When the man got out of jail, he became a pastor and a family man. That same friend he took the fall for, came back to buy the property that the pastor's church was on because he was bitter that his life did not turn out how he wanted it to and blamed the pastor who took the fall for him. He was closing the church.

Then the pastor was falsely accused of domestic violence and ended up in jail again. While in jail, he ministered to a young boy and told him not to lose hope and that he still had time to get on the right track. The young boy had not spoken to his family. He got the courage and wrote a letter to his father, acting on the pastor's encouragement.

Charges on the pastor were dropped and he was immediately discharged after the accuser came clean with the truth about her abuser.

Pastor got out of jail just in time for the benefit the church was giving to support the residence of an apartment building fire. They were going to have the benefit despite the impending closing of the church.

It turned out that the young boy was the son of the pastor's friend, the same friend he took the fall for, the same friend who was closing the church. Needless to say, that friend was eternally grateful that the pastor ministered to his son in jail and apologized for blaming him for how his life turned out. He decided to take responsibility of the part he played in his own life track.

The movie was called, "A Christmas Prayer". This movie had me in tears. It had many lessons on how someone can go from being on the wrong track to getting on the right track and then someone or a situation or an action could cause you to go back to the wrong track. The best part is that while on the wrong track, he made a difference in someone's life. He would have never met the young man if he was not falsely accused.

Perhaps we should not refer to the situation as a wrong track, but as a detour. Pastor was already on the right track.

Have you lost your way because your faith was weak? What do you have faith in?

"ATTENTION, PASSENGERS: The next train is on Track 2."

Track 2 –UNBELIEF/DISBELIEF

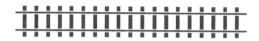

Unbelief can rip you from the track you are supposed to be on. When people see miracles happen, some believe, but some will see and still will not believe.

God gave me an amazing gift of playing piano. I hear a song and I go to the piano and play it. No teacher, just my ear. When I tell people this, it is hard for them to believe it. I will even show them that I now know how to play and they still do not believe. In the back of their minds, they are probably saying, you must have had piano lessons every week. It is a gift that I did not know I had in me.

In the movie, "Santa Clause", the character said, "I see a polar bear riding a bike, but I don't believe it. The elf said, "You are missing the point; seeing is not believing, believing is seeing."

I had a conversation with a man in a store who said he did not believe in God. I took him at his word. We were then having a discussion about another subject and he thought I did not believe what he was telling me.

Then he lifted up his right hand and said, "As God is my witness…" I was like, "Oh? Whose God are you referring to?" He could not believe that he said that and in front of a store full of people.

Some, need help with their unbelief. People have trouble believing in themselves. Some people do not believe that they can accomplish things. They believe that they are a failure.

It is really not disbelief... it is a belief in negative thoughts as opposed to believing that they can do all things.

As the song poet says in the movie "The Wiz", "Believe in yourself as I believe in you."

Let me tell you why I believe in miracles. I bought a house, working part-time, with five children. They told me I could not have children, yet I have five.

Can you think of a time/times in your life where the unbelievable happened?

At some point, we have to learn to see with not just our physical eyes, but with our spiritual eyes.

We are all born with great gifts, talents and skills, to be equipped to be on our track, and our unbelief can keep us from discovering them.

My prayer is: Father God, help me with my unbelief. I pray this for me and for you.

Are you on the right track? If no, why not? Is it because of disbelief and fear?

Track 3 – FEAR

Fear is the number one killer of dreams. Fear is so real that the Bible tell us not to fear 365 times. What are we so afraid of? Fear will have us sitting on a train that is on a track that has ended. Some will not even get on the train. Some will not drive on the highway. Some will not learn to swim.

Fear was a factor of why it took seven years to write my first book. I never in my life thought that I would be an author. I wonder what track I would have been on had I not written a book. Would I have stayed stuck at the train station? Maybe.

Fear has me driving on the highway, screaming. I hate driving. I don't even like driving up the street, let alone on the highway.

Fear of heights (acrophobia) is a big issue for me. I might have missed out on a great job opportunity, as the job I interviewed for, was on the 25th floor. I got on the elevator and was crying by the time I got to the floor.

Then they had the nerve to sit me in an office with no wall... it was all window. Were they kidding me? The interviewer said that I was the best candidate on paper, but she did not think I could take the heights. I totally agreed and ran out of there as fast as I could. I got on a different track.

Cast out fear!!! People get off track because they are scared of the schemes of whatever might be on the track that they are on.

Some would tell themselves that they cannot make it through on that track because it is too advanced.

They may even say something like "I am just me," not knowing that they are extraordinary.

Is the reason why you can't swim because you almost drowned? Is the reason why you hate relationships because you were hurt before? Is the reason why you haven't moved to the next level because it is too painful? Are you staying in the small apartment because you are too scared to buy a house. Face your fears! You are God's best. In you, holds wondrous truths, greatness, passions and even miracles that are untouched because of this thing called fear. Don't let fear take you off the track that is set before you.

One of the oldest tricks in the devil's book is to inject fear into you by reminding you of your past failures. He keeps reminding you of your past embarrassments. People would get on the wrong train at South Station and they would have to get off at the next stop, go around to the other side, and take the train back to South Station because they were on the wrong track.

Remember, God did not give you the spirit of fear, but of power, love and a sound mind. 2Timothy 1:7 (KJV)

If you are scared, it did not come from God. Don't be afraid to take a track that you don't see other people traveling on. Sometimes, in your life, there is a new track, a new direction. Even if you are scared, move forward on your track with your knees shaking.

Track 4 – ANXIETY AND DEPRESSION ARE FEAR'S TWINS

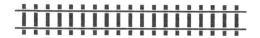

Anxiety and depression (A&D) can put a complete stop on your moving forward on your track.

People get stopped in their tracks dealing with the emotions of A&D. A&D can have you pushing people who care about you away. It will have you questioning your track.

It can keep you in dangerous situations. I didn't even realize that I was in a season of depression for many years. I slept on my couch for twenty years after I was divorced. When I was married and my ex was acting right, we would sleep together as a married couple. I kind of got used to someone sleeping next to me. When we got divorced, that part of the bed was too empty for me. I ran to the couch, since the back of the couch functioned as a person.

I took a step out of that situation. I ordered a bed online. When it came, I had my brother put the frame together. I bought the mattress that was rolled up. I decided that I was going to unroll it myself even though my son was in the other room. The mattress attacked me as it was opening up. I was almost trapped between it and the frame. LOL.

Even when I had the bed set up, it took me about a week and a half before I decided to sleep in it. You see, I was so used to sleeping on the couch. I was so depressed and accustomed to being depressed. The night I finally decided to sleep in my new bed, was the first time in years that I got the best sleep ever.

Today, I can no longer sleep on the couch. If I fall asleep on the couch, I jump up and go to bed. I am free from the couch's hold. I jumped on a fresh new track. As I got onto this track, more opportunities and more blessings arose. Since I started sleeping in my bed, my roof was replaced and my hallway and the kitchen floors were redone. What is anxiety and depression keeping you from experiencing? Most times, when someone is having an anxiety attack, it could be apprehension of trying something new. Sometimes they have anxiety when they are not doing what they are supposed to be doing. Deep down inside, people know what is right from wrong. They probably feel guilty when doing wrong and it comes out as anxiety or depression. When people feel like they are not on the right track, they get frustrated.

Depression's symptoms can have someone holding on to past hurt. It could have you all messed up because things are not going the way we think they are supposed to be going. Some require medical attention and some just need to decide that everything will be all right.

Are Anxiety and Depression keeping you off the right track?

Please, you should seek counseling to teach life coping skills. Life has triumphs and victories, but there will always be trials and tribulations. There is no such thing as a perfect track.

Getting on your right track, will decrease anxiety and depression.

Everyone has outlets to relieve stress, anxiety and depression. Mine are singing, going for walks, writing songs, writing poems, playing piano, playing pool, swimming and shooting hoop. Yes, I still go out to my driveway and shoot hoops on my own basketball hoop. I perfected shooting three-pointers by watching Steph Curry. I felt like you should know that.

Find your outlets and do them, to alleviate your stress.

I cast out fear, anxiety and depression. They have to go, in Jesus' name. Replace them with faith so that people can stay on the track that God has set before them. I pray that they don't lose focus on You and Your direction, God, but that they walk uprightly before You, following the steps that You ordered for their lives. I asked this in the name of the Lord Jesus Christ, that they don't look to the left or right, but to keep their eyes on You, oh Lord!

Philippians 4:6-7 (NIV) – Do not be anxious about anything, but in every situation, by prayer and petition, with thanksgiving, present your requests to God. 7 And the peace of God, which transcends all understanding, will guard your hearts and your minds in Christ Jesus.

Track 5 – LETTING PEOPLE TELL YOU WHAT TRACK TO BE ON

Someone told you were not good enough so you stopped going on the track toward your dream and started going on a different track. Is that you?

Did someone say you were not going to be successful at becoming a musician?

Did someone say you were too fat to be a dancer?

Did someone call you dumb or stupid?

Did you try to fit into a crowd that did not respect you, or did they reject you?

Was someone so hard on you that you retreated?

Did someone say you were not going to amount to anything and you heard it so much that you began to believe it? Is one of these questions the reason you got off track?

I have met many people who stopped doing the very thing that they were supposed to be doing.

I met a girl who was singing so beautifully under her breath. I asked her where she sang. She told me she didn't sing anymore. Apparently, she had a musician boyfriend who broke her heart, so she told herself she was not going to sing ever again.

I explained to her that singing is a gift from God and He did not give her the gift to sit on it.

I advised her to find an opportunity to sing. I told her people need to hear her voice. Singing is not only healing to her, but to others. For her, not singing is like her getting on a train that is in the train yard, immobile.

There was a time when I had a breakdown and the counselor said, "You sing. When was the last time you sang?" I could not even tell her. She told me to go home and sing in the morning and then sing at night. When I went back for my next appointment, I was a different person.

To teens, young adults and adults in touch with their inner child -- Many times, grown-ups ask you what you want to be when you grow up, and in the same breath, they tell you that you cannot accomplish said dream or that it would not make a good living.

Most grown-ups mean well and want to see you prosper, but they believe you should be doctors, lawyers, scientists and the like.

But maybe that is not the track that you are supposed to be on. Maybe you are supposed to be an artist, musician or a concierge.

Be respectful, but if you feel in your spirit what track you are supposed to be on, pursue that track.

Sometimes, at the train station, we ask the customer service desk what track our train is on and are told the wrong track.

Be careful that some people do not want to see you on the right track, they do not want to see you win. Do not be deceived or deterred.

Some people are for college, some are not. If you want to be a pediatrician, then you need to go to college. Whether your track needs college or not, you should still educate yourself with things you need to, to stay on your track.

I think some parents want you to do something. They throw college at you so that you can do something.

Are you supposed to be at the 9-5 job or are you supposed to be a travel agent? Are you supposed to go on missions, helping other countries?

For basketball players, you may have coaches being hard on you or not playing you in the big basketball game or they have favorites.

You cannot let this stop you from playing the game. Maybe they are hard on you because they know you can be better or maybe that is not the team for you.

Have you been looked over for a promotion? I have. Was it given to someone with a lower position than you? Do not be discouraged. You will get what you are supposed to have. Sometimes you need to step out of your comfort zone and go get a higher paying job.

You have teachers giving you a low grade, when you thought you did A quality work. Do not let them stop you or discourage you. Study harder.

Are you that person who only heard the word "No" your whole life? Don't get discouraged; someone will eventually say yes.

Be discerning as to who is actually trying to get you to the next level of your track or who is trying to block you from your purpose and destiny.

Staying on the right track, is ultimately *your* responsibility.

"ATTENTION, PASSENGERS: The next train is on Track 6."

Track 6 – RELATIONSHIPS

There are some who come off the track they are on, to follow someone else. They were clearly on a whole different path and then they changed just for that someone.

I know people who move to a whole other state just to be with a person. They leave their friends, family and their support system. Then the person they moved to be with left them.

Be careful about making big decisions with someone who is not really into you.

I have seen people who got off their track, made compromises, not really sure that they should have left their track, but left it anyway. And it turned out to be a disaster.

Sometimes we fall in love with someone's potential, and not the actual person. We see red flags and ignore them.

We hope that the person whom we changed our track for is willing to stay with us, ignoring the fact that you know that person to jump from track to track.

I remember telling a friend of mine, who was a social worker, that it was not a good idea to date her clients.

If a person you are dating is trying to change you, not allowing you to be yourself, they are not the ONE.

Move on.

In relationships, the ones you are supposed to be with, will be running on the same track as you willingly.

Some people's tracks are different; they decide to be on same track because of love. But the love should be reciprocated. There is nothing worse than unrequited love.

Why do we pick mediocrity? Why do we settle? Why do we go on the track that we know we are not supposed to be on? We know that the person is not good for us, so why do we stay? Why do we think that we can make the person stay on the same track as us? We are not made to be mediocre, but to soar.

Even in relationships with children and other family members, we must learn how to relate with love. In dealing with bosses, friends and associates, we must exercise respect. We have to know our own value.

Please, while you are dating, take your time to get to know the person. If they are rushing, they have an agenda. Please don't be touchy until you get to know each other and know that you will be together (true love relationship). At least learn their last name. Watch how they treat their mother and father. Listen to what conversations their family has about them.

If a person stops communicating, don't chase. Let them go. You will be okay without them.

Some people want to be married so badly that they will marry the bottom of the barrel. There are seasons in our lives where we have to be single. We have to be okay with being single. We have to be sure that our track is solid before we join onto someone else's solid track.

In relationships, the first person we should love is ourselves. We need to be able to recognize love when it is shown to us. We also need to learn how to accept love. And we also need to know when it is a façade.

Love conquers all. Perhaps we need to learn what love really is? I get the definition of love from the Bible.

1 Corinthians 13:4-9 (ESV) Love is patient, love is kind; love does not envy or boast; it is not arrogant or rude. It does not insist on its own way; it is not irritable or resentful; it does not rejoice at wrongdoing, but rejoices with the truth. It always protects, always perseveres. Love never fails.

If you are not completely sure of joining onto someone else's track, stay on your own track.

Track 7 – LOW SELF-ESTEEM

If we hear derogatory things about ourselves sometimes, we start believing them. For example, I listened to a song three times and then I could not get it out of my mind. The words were not uplifting. In speaking to people, we are quick to believe negative things that are said about us. Words can hurt us. Words are powerful.

Sometimes we stop going the way God designed us to because we think it's too hard, so hard that we get discouraged and we give up...

Is that you? I encourage you to push past the discomfort. For those who have earring holes or tattoos or had babies or weight lift, you pushed past the pain before.

For those of you who broke limbs, who got hit by a car, or have a painful illness, you have pushed past the pain. You can do that same thing on the track to your purpose. Did you know that you are fearfully and wonderfully made in the image of God. So what, you may have big eyes, a little tiny nose or you can't run as fast as others.

Everyone is born with a purpose in mind and has different jobs. It is just like every part of your body has a different job. Your eyes see, your nose smells, your legs walk etc.

People used to tease me because I wear glasses. They used to tease my "big" lips. I learned to like who I am, "four-eyed and big-lipped "and all.

Don't let someone take you off your track by telling you that you are beautiful just to get something from you for their own personal gain. The truth of the matter is you should already know that and you should love yourself enough not to fall for that game.

Low self-esteem can definitely take you off the track you are supposed to be on. A person's mind will tell them that the train is too extravagant for their simple self.

So what, you are moving slower than most? This may be the pace for you. The point is to get to know and love who you are despite your iniquities.

This is one of the lies that the enemy tells us so that we stay off the track to prosperity.

Repeat after me: I am made with purpose in mind. I am smart. I have many talents and gifts. I am valuable. I am extraordinary.

Speak these declarations until you believe them.

You should be singing the song from the song poet. Fat Joe says, "Nothing can stop me. I'm all the way up!"

The last line of a poem I wrote in my book, I'm 25, should be your motto:

The most powerful you become is when you just be yourself.

Exercise your esteem building muscle.

Building your self-esteem will set you on the right track.

Psalm 139:14 (KJV) I will praise thee; for I am fearfully and wonderfully made: marvelous are thy works and that my soul knoweth right well.

Track 8 – DISTRACTIONS

I have been procrastinating, doing everything other than writing the book. I used the excuse that I did not have time.

I had a dream that God took Solitaire away from me. I can play Solitaire for hours and hours. I literally play until my battery gets to 1% life. I play until I look up at the clock and it says 2 and 3 o'clock in the morning. Solitaire is a distraction. It was in the way of me staying on my track.

I jumped on my ex-husband's track, thinking we would be together forever. Ex-husband did not love me. He was using me. He always felt inferior to me. We were unevenly yoked. He was a distraction. Though my ex-husband was a distraction, God turned it around for my good. He put me on a better track.

A distraction can be something good that you are doing but at the wrong time. If you are distracted, you cannot hear the announcement announcing what track your train is on. What is distracting you? Is it food and lack of exercise keeping you from the track you are supposed to be on?

Is it your child calling you, wanting something to drink, or is it you having to watch football?

Or are you just being lazy?

Laziness is unprofitable. The soul of a lazy man desires, and has nothing; But the soul of the diligent shall be made rich. Proverbs 13:4 (NKJV)

It is normal to get distracted, but remember to start focusing on getting back on track.

While typing this book, I got up to stretch, then ended up in the kitchen, seasoning chicken, turning on the kettle for tea, washed a couple of dishes, when I should have been writing. I came off my track for longer than I should have. I should have done all the outside stuff prior to commencing to type. You can get distracted by doing something good. For instance, I am typing, and while I am thinking, I look around and notice a cup on the living room table. I proceed to get up and take the cup to the sink. Not only do I bring it to the sink, I will wash it, then dry and then put it away. In the meantime, my train left. And now I am going to have to wait for the next train. Distractions could be a reason why someone would be on my train instead of the train they are supposed to be on.

Other distractions are if you are angry, tired or hungry. You are not focused on what track you are supposed to be on. You may board the train on the wrong track.

This is a story about how hunger was a distraction. I went a majority of the day without eating. I sang at an event and then attempted to go out with family… They got to the event at least fifteen minutes before I did. I was trying to get on their track but got discouraged due to being hungry and tired and had on the wrong attire, as the event was outside. I turned around and went to the start of the event where I saw food. I learned that maybe I should have carried a snack and changed my attire before I attempted to meet my family or perhaps even went home instead. I got off my track trying to get on theirs.

Try carving out time to do a project. Ignore distractions during that time period. You have to do the same thing you do to get in front of the TV when a football game is coming on.

If that does not work for you, then you should do what I do and do other things and come back to the project, just don't spend a million years doing the "other things" when you are supposed to be doing that project.

Sometimes people have on headphones, music so loud blasting in their ears that they could not hear the train track being called. They can do something as simple as turning the music down or off while waiting for the train track announcement.

Smoking cigarettes and weed, doing drugs and drinking alcohol are other big distractions. In fact, it keeps you from your greatness. It can keep you from discovering just how extraordinary you are. All the paraphernalia was designed for you to do is to drown your sorrows, to forget about your troubles, but at the same time, not find out what your purpose is.

People get on the wrong track when they start stealing to support their habit. Some would rather buy drugs than eat. You were born with a purpose in mind. You will not find your purpose using drugs and smoking weed and you definitely will not find it in the bottom of a bottle. Stay focused!

Track 9 – BEING PUT UNDER PRESSURE

There are bad applications of pressure, i.e., peer pressure, why don't you drink that, why don't you smoke this, or someone telling you to go somewhere you have no business going.

I knew a person whose grandmother was Japanese. All the little kids around her way would tease her grandmother. So, in order to stay on the teasers' track, she would tease her grandmother in front of them and stopped going to her grandmother's house, around the corner from her. Then her grandmother passed away. She had so much regret because she did not get a chance to get to know her grandmother and experience her love. She went on the wrong track.

Some will know in their heart that what they are being asked to do is wrong and will do it anyway for acceptance. Lateness is added pressure. When you are rushing to catch your train, you may hear the track incorrectly. You may fall. You may forget something. I had a friend who was rushing to get to work. When at work, he noticed that he had different color shoes on. Funny, right? Doubt is added pressure. If you tell yourself that you are not going to be able to catch your train, you unconsciously tell your body to slow down.

Most pressure is what we put on ourselves. We have a tendency to be so hard on ourselves. We have to learn to give ourselves grace.

Please use the pressure application to stop a wound from bleeding out.

Please use pressure to fill up an inner tube or basketball or your car wheel. I heard this video that hit my core about the application of pressure. The gentleman said that sometimes we go through hard things because that would be the only thing to get us to move.

Many times, we stop doing things because we think it is too hard. If a body builder stops lifting weights because they thought it was too hard, they would not get muscles.

Are you on the wrong track because of pressure? You should use pressure to push you toward your purpose.

Track 10 – BEING STUCK

Are you stuck? Do you feel like you don't know where to go or what to do? Are you currently doing the same thing, expecting a different result? Everyone gets stuck from time to time. Sometimes we feel sad and hopeless due to past traumas. Sometimes we do not know who we are. Sometimes we do not know our purpose. Why were we born? When we don't know these things, we do not know where to go or what to do.

Ways to become unstuck: Step away from routine. Do something new. Get educated on something that you always wanted to do. Ask yourself who you are. Deal with your past traumas. If you need help, it is okay to seek therapy. Ask yourself what you are passionate about. Push toward pursuing that passion. Take a break!

Sometimes there is a mountain in front of you. Learn to climb OR go around it.

It is okay to pause, to make sure you did not leave anything behind or that you are still on the track that you are supposed to be on. Self-assessments are essential.

It is not okay to stay stuck. We are born to keep moving forward.

In the movie, "Cool Runnings", the Jamaican team's sled crashed short of the finish line. They picked the sled up and walked it over the finish line. Me: I ask God to open my eyes and ears to see the track (steps) that He had ordered for me. There are connecting trains. Sometimes you will miss your connecting train.

You were built for the track God set you on. It is okay to start all over. In fact, you should thank God for the opportunity to even start all over. Each new day God gives you on this side of eternity is a blessing but not to just sit on your blessed assurance and do nothing. It is an opportunity to bear fruit and push you toward finding your purpose by how you live your life.

No matter where you are on your track, God will work everything out for our good for those who love HIM. Romans 8:28 (paraphrase).

Track 11 – UNFINISHED BUSINESS

Walking and thinking, or walking and listening to music, angry about something, haven't spoken to your

brother or mother, didn't finish a task at work, attention deficit. Are you walking around aimlessly, thinking about a lot of things?

Do you have unfinished business? Did you finish that paper so you can graduate college? Did you write that book? Did you get your license? Did you put in that bid to buy that house? Did you write that business plan?

Unfinished business can put you on the wrong train, and not on the track that you are supposed to be on. Just think, if you took that training, you would have gotten that high-paying job. If you would have gotten your license, you would have received that new car.

Write a personal and/or a business vision board. Finish tasks one at a time. Make a daily to-do list.

Do not let unfinished business crowd your mind.

There are tracks that you are on and there are tracks you are supposed to be on. Get it together.

Track 12 – UNFORGIVENESS

Unforgiveness can take you off your track. Holding on to someone who wronged you keeps you on their track and not on your own track. You would probably see that person on the street and go all the way around or take another route just to avoid them.

What I am asking you to do is not easy but necessary. Forgive whoever hurt you.

The people you are holding are living their lives and have moved on. Some of the people have passed away. They can no longer apologize to you.

Sometimes someone will genuinely apologize and we will still not forgive.

For your health and well-being, you must let them go.

Let me tell you how I learned to forgive. I acknowledge that they are only human. There are no perfect people in this world.

Ephesians 6:12 For our struggle is not against flesh and blood, but against the rulers, against the authorities, against the powers of this dark world and against the spiritual forces of evil in the heavenly realms.

Everyone will hurt you, deliberately or not.

Either way, you must forgive them, and not for them, for you.

When you forgive something or someone, it does not mean that you need to have a relationship with them, especially if they did something dreadful.

Even Jesus, when he was hung on the tree, said to God, "…Father, forgive them; for they know not what they do…." Luke 23:34 (KJV)

Forgiveness will free you to see and receive blessings that you were unable to see due to unforgiveness blinders.

And God can forgive you for things you did.

FORGIVE. You will thank me later.

"ATTENTION, PASSENGERS: The next train is on Track 13."

Track 13 – PRIDEFUL

Some of us have so much pride that we will not ask for directions. Then we end up somewhere we have no business being. Someone who knows where to go is telling us where to go, we deem them not credible and we should have listened to them. Some don't know where to go and just hop on any train.

Prideful people only think about self. They always expect everyone to serve them and don't want to do the serving. No one likes someone who thinks that they are superior to others.

Prideful people think they know everything. When we know everything, we cannot learn anything.

Prideful people have the "me" syndrome. We have to know that it is not always going to be about us.

Life is all about helping one another. If you are only thinking about yourself, it leads to destruction (Proverbs 16:18).

If you think that you are the smartest one ever, you are going to be the smartest all by yourself.

Please do not be this way. Admit when you do not know, because no one on this earth knows everything.

We are all imperfect. It is okay to admit that you need help.

Repeat after me: I DO NOT KNOW IT ALL. I AM A WORK IN PROGRESS!

Pride will keep you from the right track.

Humility comes before honor. (Proverbs 18:12)

Pride should not be on your track.

There is nothing better than the track to your purpose.

Please humble yourselves.

Track 14 – WHAT ARE YOU CHASING, MONEY OR PURPOSE?

You should be chasing purpose. I am witness that if you follow purpose, the money will come.

Story time: I told my brother and his wife one February, that I was going to visit them in Virginia in August.

My sister-in- law asked every month if I had the money to come yet. I told her no, but I was still coming.

At the end of July, a friend of mine told me that the credit union was having a promotion, 0 percent down and 0 percent interest loan. I went to the credit union and applied for the loan. I got it and took myself and my five children to Virginia.

Even writing my books, who had publishing money? Not me. But the money came. You see, the money needs someplace to go.

I needed a car. Had no money in my account for a car. Got the car for FREE!

Another story: I watched a movie about a girl whose mother left her and her father. Her father was a rich workaholic. He left a credit card for the daughter and told her to buy what she wanted. He worked so much and didn't have time for her.

He bought her a convertible top car. She was longing to spend time with her father, but all he did was work, work, work. She longed for his attention and didn't get it. She started drinking and driving. She eventually crashed her new car and was put into rehab.

Her father came from a business meeting out of the country and heard on the answering service that his daughter was in a rehab.

He went to the rehab and asked his daughter what happened. He proceeded to tell her that he gave her everything that money could buy. She said, "You did not give me love." I was crying like a baby.

Are you on the wrong track because you are chasing the money?

Chasing money first, is like putting the cart before the horse.

Get on the track to your purpose and watch the money come.

Track 15 – DON'T WORRY

The Bible says when you worry, you don't really believe that God will take care of any situation you present to Him.

In this day and age, we worry about everything. Sometimes it could be something as little as 'do these shoes match with my outfit?' Worrying can blind you from seeing opportunities. Worrying is exhausting and can cause health issues and stress and wrinkles.

We have to realize that it is okay to not be in control. Many of us carry the weight of the world on our shoulders, and then wonder why we cannot handle it. I don't know if you know this, but you are not equipped to carry the weight of the world. Why don't we leave that to God? He can handle it and your burdens too. Can you picture a time when you worried about something, and then it was eventually resolved? Was your worrying worth it? I am guessing it was not.

We must replace our worrying with determination. If you are determined to do something or go somewhere, you have no time to worry.

Like the song poet, Bobby McFerrin, says, "Don't worry, be happy!"

Hakuna Matata, people! (Swahili for no worries)

Track 16 – TIME AND WAITING

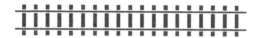

Remember, in South Station, there is a big Megatron that shows the train schedules. If you get to the station forty-five minutes before your train departure time, you would have to wait for your train, to be on the track to your destination.

We live in a microwave society, where everyone wants things fast, fast, fast.

Some things take time. When you plant a seed, you will not see it bud the next day. When you put food in the oven, it would not be cooked in 5 minutes. On your track, sometimes you will just have to wait.

"...Everything is made beautiful in its time.."
Ecclesiastes 3:11 (NKJV)

Let me tell you a story:

Two of my sisters and I were in three different cars, going to the same destination. Two of us were going to drop our cars off and hop into one sister's car. One of my sisters was behind me. The other sister went another route.

I was behind a new driver who stopped on a whim, even when there was no stop sign or stoplight. I turned off the path to take a shortcut. Little did I know, the city had closed that shortcut. I had to come back out and back onto the path that I was originally on. It took me a long time to get onto the path because there were a lot of passing cars.

My other sister, who was behind me, continued on the path that I turned from. She was now in front of me.

Needless to say, the sisters made it to the destination before I did and had to wait on me to meet them.

I should have just stayed behind the new driver until I found an opportunity to pass them, because the street did eventually turn from one lane to two lanes. I was impatient.

I thought I had a great idea which backfired. I came off the track that was set before me thinking I knew better. I should have waited.

Were you driving and there was someone driving slowly in front of you and you found the opportunity to go another direction, only to find that the person still ended up in front of you, like I did?

Or

Have you ever gotten out of a long line in the supermarket to a shorter one, only to find out that you had to wait because the cashier was doing a price check?

The long line that you were in finished first. Bummer. The moral of the story is stay on your patience track. If you are not sure on what decision to make, wait. If you are not sure of how to deal with a person or situation, wait.

We must learn to wait. Have patience.

We must learn to take our time.

Sometimes your track is being prepared and it will take time to fix it just for you. We don't want to settle or just jump on any track. Do we?

"ATTENTION, PASSENGERS: The next train is on Track 17."

Track 17 – DISAPPOINTMENT

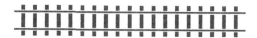

Did disappointment turn you away from the track you were supposed to be on? Some do not handle disappointment well and it will cause them to walk away from a track, rather than cooling down from disappointment.

People will disappoint you. Situations will disappoint you. Please don't let disappointment make you give up. Disappointment can lead to jealousy, and bitterness can lead you on a track to a jail cell. Have you watched the news lately? There is a lot of violence due to disappointment, jealousy, bitterness and the like.

Are you jealous? There should be no reason why you should be jealous of anyone. Everyone has a track. People are on their track, getting what they are supposed to get. You can be on your own track, getting what is on your own track. We should be happy for people when they get blessings on their track. If we are looking at other people and their track, we may miss the blessings that are on our own track.

Why are you bitter? Someone may have hurt you so badly that it has scarred your heart. Bitterness can eat away at you and can definitely take you off your track. Bitterness can even have people run from you because you spew negativity. Bitterness needs surgery, kind of like taking out an embedded tooth. Bitterness can also cause health problems. Some people do not even know that they are bitter. Again, self-assessments are in order. You should ask yourself, "How am I doing?"

You may meet someone who encourages you and loves you back onto the right track. I remember going to counseling and was complaining about what my ex did to me, he did this and he did that. She said I know that is what he did, but how about you?

I was like, me? Excuse me? What do you mean, me?

She said it again. What part did you play in all of that was going on? I was so busy looking at his track that I neglected to look at my own.

I had to wrestle through my emotions so that I could move forward in my track because I became stuck. Disappointment, jealousy and bitterness were blocking my track. I decided to deal with my feelings and move forward.

There were buttons that my ex knew how to push to get to me riled up and I decided to change my buttons. I finally started to see my track.

Am I disappointed in myself? Am I jealous? Am I bitter?

Personally, I am not.

But are you? Figure out the root and deal with them.

Therapy is not a bad idea.

Track 18 – ANGER, BUT SIN NOT

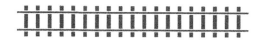

Becoming angry can throw us off track if we let it.

People can make you angry. Hunger will make you angry. We can be angry with ourselves because we cannot complete something.

If you are angry with a person, ask yourself why? What did this person do to make you angry?

Remember, people are not perfect. They will anger you. After you assess the reason, most times, it is something you just need to talk through. If that doesn't work, count down from 10 to 1, sllllowllly.

If you are hungry, eat. Nothing worse than being chemically imbalanced.

If you are angry at yourself, don't be so hard on yourself. Remember to apply grace.

The Bible says anger but sin not? You may be mad at someone and hold the very someone who is on the track you are supposed to be on. Find ways to diffuse anger i.e., exercise, punch a punching bag or go for a walk.

I had to ask myself questions. Am I still angry at that person who hurt me to my core? Or am I still angry that I did not get that job? Remember, this and other emotions affect you.

Protect your peace.

Peace be your track.

Track 19 – ROAD BLOCKS

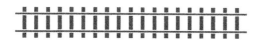

There will be road blocks.

Some road blocks keep you safe. Construction workers may block a road while they fix a road (track).

There could be a cliff beyond the road block.

A road block can also be an illness.

I had asthma for a majority of my life. I realized I never learned how to breathe properly after being delivered from asthma. I was so used to breathing incorrectly or not being able to breathe at all.

I went to a voice center and took voice lessons to learn how to breathe. I even had a bad habit of waiting until I got to the top of the stairs I was walking up before I took a breath and was wondering why I was dizzy. Asthma kept me from playing high school basketball. I ended up in JROTC instead. I wonder if I would have been a basketball star if I didn't have asthma.

I do miss playing ball.

Another road block can be that you were not listening when your track was being announced.

Yes, being rebellious is a big road block. Why do we not listen to our gut, intuition, the little man inside, some might call it the Holy Spirit?

Stinking thinking can be a road block. If you think negatively all the time, you will block your blessing. Whatever negativity you are thinking you should do, do the opposite. Procrastination is also a road block. If you know you are supposed to be writing a book, get to it. I was guilty of this. Sometimes we do more talking about it instead of moving on it. My father always tells me to stop naming myself "I'm gonna" and start doing what I say I was going to do.

Another road block can be that you expect your track to be perfect.

Your track will never be perfect, as we live in an imperfect world. We all fall short. No one is perfect.

Do we even know where we are going? Where do you see yourself in five years? What are you going to do to get there?

These are not rhetorical questions. Answering these questions provokes thought.

Another road block can be your good-for-nothing significant other. You know you are not supposed to be with them anyway. Show them to the door. Some people can't go where God is trying to take you.

Sure, you will make mistakes {get on the wrong train}, but there will always be a way to get back on track.

For those of you who believe in God, sometimes we doubt what He tells us to do or go, and go our own way. We get mad if our way produces a bad result.

Sometimes you have to go back to make things right. Going backwards is not always bad.

At South Station, when a person got on a wrong train, they got off the train at the next stop and went around to the other side and waited for the next train back to the destination that they veered off from. Sometimes we know that decision we are making is the wrong one, yet we go with it. Some feel that nudge and ignore the signs, thinking up an excuse to justify their bad decision.

When you are told don't touch the stove, why do we touch it anyway? When the answer is B on a test, why do you second guess yourself and put C?

We have to search ourselves to figure out why we do these things. We want to do it our own way. If someone told you the right way, why would you decide to go the opposite direction? Is it because you didn't want to admit you were wrong to that person?

Bad choices can take you off the positive track. Your choice to eat badly can land you in the hospital. Sometimes people think that they are blocked because they end up on a track less traveled.

I don't use profanity, I don't drink, I don't smoke, and that is typically not the norm. This typically keeps me on a track less traveled.

Sometimes we are supposed to be on a track less traveled. Keep an open mind.

Many people use a GPS, which means Global Positioning System. I call it God's Planforus System or God's Purpose System.

When you take a wrong turn, recalibrate.

Do not give up!

"ATTENTION, PASSENGERS: The next train is on Track 20."

Track 20 – SIDETRACKS

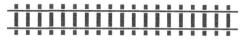

Sometimes your DREAMS give you a glimpse of your track:

4/20/2021 – I asked God whether I am good with Him, walking on the right path.

I went to sleep and had a dream that I was walking down this dimly lit path. I had on a white robe. All of a sudden, I felt warmth on my hand and a Presence next to me. There was a Whisper. I heard, "Yes, you are on the right track. Do not look to the left or right. Keep walking, straight that way." (He was pointing to the path in front of me.) God also revealed other things that I prayed for on my track. He sensed a little dismay on my part. He said, "Do not worry, everyone you have ever prayed for is also on the right track despite what their journey looks like."

I woke up with such a joy in my heart, to know that I am on the right track and so are all the family, friends, and people I was asked to pray for. They are on the right track, too, and I also prayed for YOU at the beginning of this book.

I had another dream, that I went to a concert with a group of people. Transportation dropped us in front of the building with no itinerary. The building had many concert halls. The two people who decided to follow me to find out our destination, had no idea where to go or who to ask. They were no help in finding it out.

I asked a worker, who had no idea what concert or where. He sent me to the front desk at the front of the building. I got to the customer service desk. There was a lady there, claiming to be me. As I showed my license, the imposter scurried off.

The customer service representative proceeded to give me and the two people who were with me tickets but said that it was hopeless to go to the concert because we were late. She said that we most likely missed the whole concert. We went to the concert anyway. When we got there, the concert hadn't started yet.

The lessons from the dreams:

Be around people who are more informed about and are willing to help get information.

Ask the right person what you need. You can't ask a janitor at the train station what track your train is on.

There is always going to be someone who will try to kill, steal and destroy you.

People who are supposed to help you and don't, can also deter you from your track.

Be determined to stay the course.

Do you have dreams? My suggestion is to write them down. They maybe key to you staying on track.

TRACK SURVEYS

I conducted a survey to see if people became what they dreamed of being in their youth.

Subject #1 said she wanted to be a medical secretary but school was a challenge for her. She said that she wishes she would have chosen differently because she feels like she is just living to work. She is currently a clerk typist which is really close to what she wanted to be, minus the medical part.

Subject #2 said he wanted to be a fireman. As he got older, he realized that being a fireman needed a fearless requirement that he did not have. Though he did not become a fireman, he is happy being a realtor, father and husband.

Subject #3 said he wanted to be a professional athlete, then he wanted to be a bus driver. He is a now a plumber and became one because an apprenticeship came up, and he wanted the pay. He watched his parents pay plumbers top dollar. Plumbing was not his dream job, but he makes a good living. He enjoys helping people close to him or giving advice.

No wrong decisions, but you just pay consequences, good or bad.

In "Gulliver's Travels", the guy kept saying, "You will never make it." Are you talking yourself off the right track, with words like, "I can't?" Are you allowing people's words to stop you from going for your passion?

Are you forcing yourself on someone else's track? Let me tell you, if you stay on your track, God will send people who are supposed to be on your track.

An example of who is supposed to be on your track, ends up on your track:

I had a friend I had known since we were six years of age. She moved off the street we lived on and onto her track.

I went on my track. We went through life's ups and downs. She became an author during her track and I did too. Then we started running into each other at different places.

One day, I went to the park where concerts were playing, because a sister friend told me she was going to meet me there.

Since I know lots of people, I knew I would be all right to walk around and bump into people I know.

Well, I bumped into this friend while waiting for my sister friend. We even took a picture that day.

It turned out the sister friend I was supposed to meet ended up not coming at all. If it was not for my sister friend, I would not have been at the park.

I was about to stay at home.

Fast forward to today. That friend and I decided to run a workshop for young girls, informing them of sexual assault awareness and self-confidence, self-esteem building and self-love.

See, God had our tracks collide so that we can minister to young girls.

One particular workshop, we went to set up, then we found out that girls did not sign up for the workshop. We were in that room praying. I asked God to send girls into the workshop, quicken them to get up and come in so we could pour into them and He will get the glory. I also asked the Lord to send an angel.

We asked four girls if they wanted to come in. We then went into the workshop room and we waited. As we were talking and waiting in the room, my friend and I were thanking God for the girls we ministered to in previous workshops.

We heard and saw three of the girls leave. We were saying how those three girls were going to miss out on this life-changing workshop.

We kept talking, and then, all of a sudden, in walked the fourth girl. And you would not believe what her name was. Her name was Angel. God sent an Angel, literally.

We ministered to her and she poured out some truths. She told us that she was going to be a writer, especially, poetry.

She was an answered prayer. I asked God to send an angel. I didn't even know why I asked for an angel that day. We ministered to one another.

I tell girls not to chase people because, as you are walking on your track, God will send people to be with you, just as he put my friend and me together, to create this workshop and pour into the girls.

This day was fulfilling. It made me full!

.

CONCLUSION AND PURPOSE DESTINATION

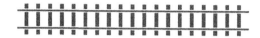

These questions need answers.

Are you on the right track? If not, how will you get back on track?

In visiting the tracks in this book, did you see yourself in one or more of these tracks, whether favorable or unfavorable?

What is your purpose?

How will you find out what our purpose is? What are your passions? What are your gifts? Your gifts and passions will connect you to your purpose.

Where are you going? Who is leading you/who are you following? What are your goals? And most importantly, who are you?

For a long time, I did not know who I was, where I was going, and was living life just to live it. Though I read the Bible, sang gospel songs and went to church periodically during my life, I felt that I was driftwood, going wherever the wind blew.

Though, at South Station, I never got on the wrong train track, but I did get off at the wrong stops and had to reroute.

I am glad that, in life, you have an opportunity to have do-overs.

I found a Leader to follow. This is not a religious statement. I found God and agreed to follow Him. I am no longer on an aimless track. I am here to tell you that God wants to lead you to the right track because He knows what is best for you. After all, He is the One who created you. If you had a furniture piece that you needed to put together, you would use the instructions that came with it.

God has a wonderful plan for your life. He wants to order your steps into your destiny and purpose.

God is leading you daily if you let Him.

We have to kill the noise and focus.

Everyone is born with a purpose. If you do not know what your purpose is, look back at your life and see what you have been doing well. If you are good with dealing with people, you may be a counselor or even a minister. If, when you look back at your life and still do not know what your purpose is, do something new.

Use the GPS –God's Purpose Systems.

Everyone was born with greatness. Everything that you need to live this life is in you. Search yourself. Get to know how extraordinary you are and that you are enough.

When I wrote my book of my life story, Music is the Key, I recognized a pattern, a track. People come to me for prayer, for encouragement, for worship and even for a joke because they need to laugh...

I had a gentleman say, "I heard you are the author who hears from God."

I had another lady call me a hope pusher. I am not perfect. In fact, I am still battling some of the obstacles mentioned in this book. We do live in an imperfect world.

I do know that I am actually walking in my purpose and that I am on my right track.

Learn how to do everything with Love.

I ask the question again, "ARE YOU ON THE RIGHT TRACK?"

Psalm 37:23 (KJV) The steps of a good man are ordered by the Lord, and He delights in his way.

Proverbs 4:18 (NIV) The path of the righteous is like the morning sun, shining ever brighter till the full light of day.

Made in the USA
Columbia, SC
21 July 2023

20707065R00055